The purpose of this study guide is to provide supplemental educational material. It is not intended as a substitute or replacement of RISING OUT OF HATRED.

Published by SuperSummary, www.supersummary.com

ISBN – 9781701083202

For more information or to learn about our complete library of study guides, please visit http://www.supersummary.com

Please submit any comments, corrections, or questions to: http://www.supersummary.com/support/

TABLE OF CONTENTS

Rising Out of Hatred: The Awakening of a Former White Nationalist (2018) is a biography of disavowed white nationalist Derek Black, authored by Pulitzer Prize-winning journalist Eli Saslow.

Derek is a former white nationalist wunderkind. Derek is the son of former Ku Klux Klan Grand Wizard and *Stormfront* online hate group creator, Don Black, and the godson of former Ku Klux Klan Grand Wizard, white supremacist politician, and notorious public figure, David Duke. Derek's parents remove him from public school and groom him to be a rising star in the movement through homeschooling, white nationalist conferences, and familial relationships. By age 19, Derek is famous in the white nationalist community for his presence on *Stormfront*, his AM radio show, cable news appearances, and lectures reforming the movement from its violent past into mainstream ideology.

Derek leaves his family and their ideology for the first time to attend a progressive liberal arts college where he befriends immigrants, Jews, and LGBTQ students. He forms personal relationships with them and for the first time views members of these groups as human beings rather than abstract concepts. Derek's friendship with nonwhites forces him to recognize their viewpoints as legitimate and question his own long-held ideology.

When a classmate unearths Derek's identity as a prominent white nationalist, the college community turns against Derek. He is lonely and isolated. When an Orthodox Jewish friend invites Derek to Shabbat dinner with a group of students, Derek embraces the social opportunity and returns every week. This begins the lengthy process of Derek's

2

classmates dissuading him from his white nationalist ideology. Derek's views shift not through debate or confrontation, but through friendship. As his friendships with the diverse group of students deepen, his commitment to an ideology that excludes them weakens. A friend presents him with information refuting the pseudoscience behind much of his beliefs, and he publicly disavows white nationalist ideology.

White nationalism is the glue that holds Derek's family together. When Derek disavows the ideology, he causes an irreparable schism in his family. He is no longer welcome in his childhood home; *Stormfront* members spew vitriol at him; his interactions with his father consist only of verbal jabs. Derek moves from Florida to the Midwest, then the Northeast, and as white nationalism engulfs mainstream politics in the run-up to the 2016 presidential election, Derek speaks publicly about his experiences and the dangers of white nationalism. Simultaneously, Don and Duke are mentoring Richard Spencer and other rising stars in white nationalism as racial politics engulf the United States before and after the 2016 presidential election. Derek and his family are now adversaries in a national battle. They do not engage as a family or even socially. Each works to spread their ideological message and defeat the other in the court of public opinion. Each views the contest as vital for the future of the United States, and each is committed to defeating the other.

Introduction-Chapter 3

Introduction Summary

The formative years of Derek's life are a grooming by his family to become the future leader of white nationalism in the United States. Derek creates white nationalism marketing tools for the popular website *Stormfront*, conducts a daily radio show, and lectures at white nationalism conferences on how to bring the ideology into the mainstream. Derek becomes one of the most famous white nationalists in the country. In Derek's last interview, in 2013, "he disavowed his beliefs and apologized for everything he'd done" (1), then disappears. Eli Saslow finds Derek several years later attending graduate school under a new legal name and requests an interview. Derek initially rebukes Saslow, but in the summer of 2016 when Saslow tries again, Derek accepts his interview offer because he feels "implicated by current events, sometimes even culpable" (2). Saslow then spends hundreds of hours with Derek, his friends, and family members to understand his radical transformation from white nationalist wunderkind to progressive in vocal opposition to his former ideology.

Chapter 1 Summary: "The Great White Hope"

At a 2008 meeting of Klansmen and neo-Nazis, the infamous white supremacist Duke states, "The future of our movement is to become fully mainstream" before introducing "the leading light" of such movement, 19-year-old Derek (6). After leading the Ku Klux Klan for more than a decade, Derek's father Don founded the white supremacist website *Stormfront*. Derek's mother Chloe was previously married to Duke, who is Derek's godfather. Saslow states, "Duke acted as Derek's mentor and godfather, sometimes referring to Derek as 'the heir'" (7). Derek commands such reverence from the white nationalist community because, while his beliefs are the same as other white nationalists-that the United States is a country for those they deem white and all others should be forcibly removed-his rhetoric is more statesmanlike. Saslow explains that at the meeting "instead of basing his public arguments on emotion or explicit prejudice, he spoke mostly about what he believed to be the facts of racial science, immigration, and a declining white middle class" (7). Derek's goal is to normalize white nationalist ideas to become more acceptable in mainstream society. The meeting's attendees believe white nationalism will ignite a political revolution and that Derek will lead that revolution.

Don and Chloe remove Derek from public school after third grade because they believe the West Palm Beach public schools are "overwhelmed by an influx of Haitians and Hispanics" (10-11). They describe his subsequent schooling as "unschooled," and focus more on ideology than curriculum. Saslow states, "He stayed home during the day and worked on a curriculum largely of his own creation while Don monitored Stormfront [...] Derek taught himself basic coding and built the Stormfront children's website" (11). As Derek matures, he joins Don in interviews on *USA Today*, Nickelodeon, and NBC.

In 2008 Derek successfully wins election as a Palm Beach County Republican committeeman by canvassing and discussing issues with voters. He seldom mentions race explicitly. Instead, he discusses issues such as urban crime and outsourced middle-class jobs while maintaining race as subtext. He lectures to other white nationalists that the ideology can achieve mainstream success only if it adopts a vocabulary that sanitizes the ideology and distances it from its violent history. Derek explains, "[W]hite nationalists [are] not fighting *against* minority rights but fighting *for* rights of their own" (13).

When the Palm Beach County Republican committee learns of Derek's racial views, they vote to prevent him from holding his elected seat. Derek challenges this action and tries to claim his seat at a committee meeting. The fiasco draws the attention of national news and while Derek does not reclaim his elected position, his handling of it on national media catapults him and his ideology to the forefront of national politics. Don notices, "[W]hite nationalism was not just some fringe ideology held by a small number of extremists but in fact the 'natural impulse' for a majority of whites in America" (15).

In 2010 Derek continues his quest "to overturn our social order and replace it" by starting a white nationalist AM radio show titled the *Derek Black Show* (18). The show is successful and expands from two days per week to five. In the midst of the show's success, Derek transfers from community college to New College of Florida, "the state's honors college, ranked as both the most affordable and the top liberal arts school in the state" (22), with a majority white student-body, but also a reputation for being politically progressive, LGBTQ-friendly, and pot-friendly.

Chapter 2 Summary: "Have You Seen This Man?"

Derek is lost on his way to New College of Florida. He meets Juan Elias, also lost navigating to New College. Juan is a Peruvian immigrant from Miami. Derek ignores his white nationalist instincts and partners with Juan to find his way to campus. They share a dorm building and attend orientation together. Saslow says of Derek, "Even if he thought people who looked like Juan were ruining the country, he also believed that in one-on-one interactions it was always best to be polite and kind" (25). Derek and Juan would remain friends throughout their tenure at New College. At New College, Derek adopts a dual identity: reading social justice posts in the New College forum and befriending culturally diverse classmates, then sneaking away to record his white nationalist radio show with his father and complain of a "minority takeover." When befriending Matthew Stevenson, an Orthodox Jew, Derek reasons that while he may be a usurper, he is also likeable. Saslow notes, "[G]radually he went from keeping his political convictions quiet on campus to actively disguising them" (30).

At orientation, Derek meets Rose. They are attracted to each other and discuss dating until she tells Derek she is Jewish. Derek had spent hours discussing "the Jewish Question" on *Stormfront*. The question is simple: "Should Jews be considered whites or outsiders?" (32). On *Stormfront* Derek said, "Jews are the cause of all the world's strife and misery" (32). Derek's relationships with Rose and Matthew are undercutting his beliefs on Jews, formulated over a lifetime of indoctrination divorced from meaningful interaction with actual Jews. Derek describes Rose as sweet and unassuming. One of very few Jews in Arkansas, her father joined a liberal and inclusive interfaith congregation. To Derek's surprise, "[t]he mission of the congregation was not to plot some great, multicultural takeover of the white race but simply to 'serve as a focal point of Jewish life in our small corner of the world'" (34). Being a Jew in Arkansas made Rose feel alien and weird, but around Derek she feels comfortable and accepted. Derek conceals his ideology from Rose and they continue their relationship, but it intensifies Derek's internal ideological conflict. Saslow explains, "[D]ating a Jew felt to Derek like a double betrayal—first and foremost of his own beliefs, and then also of Rose, who had no idea about his history or his racial convictions" (35).

Derek's dual identities increasingly conflict as the semester continues and he continues to gain prominence within white nationalism. Eventually, "it felt to him as if both identities were eating up ever more space—his fame expanding within the movement, his private relationships deepening—and a conflict between them seemed inevitable" (38). His white nationalist foundations remain firm because his background convinces him that "[w]hite nationalism wasn't just a fringe racist movement but something much more forceful and dangerous: a foundational concept embedded in the American DNA" (40).

Abraham Lincoln believed slaves should be freed, but also that "the white race" was superior; Thomas Jefferson, another abolitionist, also believed "the two races" could not exist under the same government. Derek maintains his white nationalist ideology amidst continual rebukes, both internal and external, because of his belief that white nationalism is a foundational element of white American society. Derek reasons that it is easy for white Americans to embrace racial diversity when it doesn't cost them anything, but when white Americans' prosperity begins to falter, they will again recede to racial identity politics to protect their dwindling resources and privilege. Derek ends his first semester at New College hoping someone discovers his public personality. A classmate grants his wish during winter break. An email on the New College forum states, "Derek Black [...] White supremacist, radio host... New College Student???" (45).

Chapter 3 Summary: "I'm Not Running Away"

Tom McKay finds Derek on a Southern Poverty Law Center ("SPLC") website about far-right extremists while completing his senior thesis and exposes him via the New College forum. Within minutes, the forum thread amasses hundreds of responses and becomes the most active forum thread in the college's history. The principal issue on the forum thread discusses the appropriate response to hate speech and figures like Derek. This issue would engulf the political left and the nation in ensuing years. The forum is debating whether to exclude Derek from social and academic life or to try to alter his ideology by including him in their diverse community. Derek reads every forum post. He doesn't experience the relief he expected. He instead feels sadness over his lost friendships.

Several days later, Duke visits Derek in Munich. Most European countries have banned Duke because of his prominence as a white supremacist, so he lives in Austria. He risks arrest in Germany but wants to see Derek. Duke explains to Derek that he endured a comparable situation in college when he began speaking publicly about white supremacy. Most of Duke's classmates hated him, but his public speeches developed a following and made him a public figure. Duke reasons that Derek may follow a similar path. After their conversation, Derek reads the forum thread and "instead of feeling just hurt and vulnerable, he began to feel angry, even inspired" (60). Derek decides to return to New College and redouble his commitment to white nationalism, recruit classmates, and invite white nationalists to speak. He also decides to host "an international conference for *Stormfront* members on verbal tactics to out-argue 'anti-whites'" (60).

The New College administration debates removing Derek from the college, but concludes that if Derek doesn't threaten anyone's safety, his situation is a "student-life matter" and they cannot end his enrollment. No longer welcome living on campus, Derek rents an apartment off-campus. Some students advocate reaching out to Derek, but most practice total rejection. Some students argue, "Ignore Derek. Heckle him. Make him feel uncomfortable. 'Do not make eye contact or make him feel acknowledged at all. Make him as irrelevant as his ideology'" (66). Some students physically attack Derek. Derek spends the semester isolated, lonely, and fearful.

In the Summer of 2011, Derek hosts his first *Stormfront* conference in the Smoky Mountains of Tennessee. Hundreds of white nationalists welcome Derek with rousing applause. They believe the political moment is right for the spread of their ideology and Derek is their leader. The country is months from a presidential election in which they hope the nation's first black president will be unseated, and Donald Trump is rousing racial sentiments by insinuating that President Obama is a Kenyan-born Muslim rather than an American citizen. Saslow explains, "Don and Derek didn't much care about the legitimacy of Obama's birth certificate, but they were buoyed by the fact that by mimicking white nationalist rhetoric, Trump had amassed a massive following on the far right" (70-71). Derek tells the crowd at his conference, "It's time to adopt an attack strategy and take the moral high ground" and to stick to the message of white genocide because it "demoralizes/embarrasses anti-whites" (71). Days after returning to college from his conference, Derek receives an invitation from his Orthodox Jewish friend Matthew to attend Shabbat dinner that Friday night.

Introduction-Chapter 3 Analysis

For most of his life, Don and Chloe shelter Derek within the white nationalist community. Rather than allow him to receive opposing viewpoints and experience diverse cultures, they remove him from school to indoctrinate him in their ideology. The Blacks are antisocial shut-ins who refuse to interact with the multicultural neighborhood around them, which they see as hostile. Derek is intelligent, but his parents do not expose him to anything that would make him question the racial pseudoscience and ideology espoused by his social network of white supremacists. Derek accepts this as dogma.

When Derek arrives at New College, he meets racial, ethnic, and religious minorities for the first time. To his surprise, he likes them. They are nothing like what he expected. This creates an internal conflict in Derek between his indoctrinated ideology and his intellect, which is telling him what he learned as a child is wrong. It is Derek's politeness and openness toward others, qualities that have made him a rising star in white nationalism, that allows him to form personal relationships with diverse individuals, which permits his ideological doubts to form. If Derek was a brash, unhinged ideologue, he would not be able to befriend the people who influence him to abandon his ideology. As Derek's internal conflict grows, he increasingly wants his classmates to discover his white nationalism because he wants to publicly confront his internal hypocrisy and reclaim his identity—either as a committed white nationalist or as whatever he is becoming. When someone exposes him, Derek initially strengthens his commitment to white nationalism.

Chapters 4-6

Chapter 4 Summary: "Push the Rock"

Matthew hosts a small nondenominational group of students for Shabbat dinner every Friday. It began as a way for the only two practicing Jews in a very secular school to share their faith but grew into "a social circle all its own" (74). Matthew wants to use the weekly dinners to influence Derek's thinking. He doesn't want to confront Derek's ideology. Instead, he uses nonjudgmental inclusion to build a relationship and softly erase Derek's preconceived notions of those he considers enemies. Matthew says, "The goal was really just to make Jews more human for him" (81). Not everyone welcomes Derek at the dinners. Several participants stop attending and Matthew's roommate, Allison Gornik, hides in her room when Derek attends. The first dinner with Derek ends in mutual respect, with an implicit agreement that they won't press him on white nationalism if he forgets his beliefs during dinner. It contradicts Derek's "stay on the offensive" mantra (82), but permits him a less solitary campus.

Derek continues attending Matthew's Shabbat dinners and reengaging with the campus. He confronts new perspectives and questions many of his assumptions. To his fellow students though, his presence on campus is still a problem, reflective of broader racial issues at New College. Student activists arrange a shutdown with rallies and a speaker from the SPLC. Derek hides in the back of a rally and listens to his classmates voice opposition to transphobic statements, lack of diversity, institutional racism, and Derek. Saslow writes, "For a brief moment, he wondered: If this many smart people were so affronted by his beliefs, could they all be wrong?" (93).

Chapter 5 Summary: "Solid and Unshakable"

As he ages, Derek's father Don notices mistakes he has made in his quest for a white-only United States. He believes he was too confrontational, made too many enemies, and should have worked more from within the system. He sees a better approach in Derek, who is the embodiment of the approachable, political class of white supremacist.

Don discovered white nationalism as a teenager in the 1960s after reading *Our Nordic Race*, which states, "[t]he line of conflict is found wherever our civilization comes into contact with the belligerent and aggressive nations of the colored world" (101). The book spoke to Don and he continued reading white supremacist writings. After writing to several far-right organizations, he received copies of a newspaper called *White Power* and dozens of buttons from the National Socialist White People's Party. He used the materials to organize at his high school and attracted the attention of the FBI, who visited Don's house. Don's parents were concerned, not because they disagreed with his racial opinions, but they believed "just because the 'colored' sign had come off one of the water fountains at Gilbert's Drug Store on the downtown square didn't mean the white race was beginning its slow march toward extinction" (102). Don's parents sent him to a psychiatrist.

Don secured his future in the white supremacist movement when he drove with Duke and another young white supremacist, Joseph Paul Franklin, to a gathering of Nazis and white supremacists in Arlington, Virginia. Saslow writes, "Together they would come to define the white supremacy movement for the next several decades, but now they were three teenagers in Duke's family car" (103). During the car ride, they discussed their racial theories, traded book recommendations, and bonded. When they arrived in Arlington, "Don no longer felt like a lone extremist searching for answers. He was part of a movement, a soldier for a cause" (105). Duke returned to Louisiana State University and began his political rise; Franklin returned home and began planning what would be 15 murders in an attempt to start a race war; Don went back to Alabama and found his future in the pages of *Our Nordic Race*, which states white supremacy is "[a] problem to be solved by the cold process of intellect" (106).

Don went on to work on the gubernatorial campaign of a segregationist Ku Klux Klan member who once bombed a black church, then became the Grand Wizard of the Ku Klux Klan, and later tried to overthrow the sovereign government of Dominica to establish a whites-only colony. Don was convicted of a crime for the attempted overthrow and sentenced to federal prison, where he learned computer science, which he would subsequently use to help Duke in his gubernatorial campaign and to create *Stormfront*, the most sophisticated white supremacist organizing tool in history.

Chapter 6 Summary: "A Million Questions"

Matthew's roommate Allison no longer locks herself in her room during Shabbat dinner, but she still won't speak to Derek directly. However, she can't help but engage with Derek when they find themselves on a small sailboat together with few other passengers. To her dismay, Allison enjoys talking to Derek. A psychology major, people fascinate Allison. She tells a friend, "I'm wicked curious about the kid" (118). Allison and Derek continue seeing each other—having discussions, going on adventures, going to dances, and bonding emotionally. Like Derek's other relationships at New College, there is a mutual implicit agreement not to discuss white nationalism. Allison questions herself though, as she falls for Derek. She explains to her mother, "I'm really conflicted [...] Even if I could have some direct, positive impact, I'm not sure it is morally okay to befriend someone like this" (123). She asks herself why she is making Derek's life more pleasant instead of challenging his beliefs.

Derek is infatuated with Allison and increasingly conflicted about white nationalism. On Allison's insistence, they discuss white nationalism. They prioritize making the discussions noncombative and civil, and Allison begins "to unspool some of the questions that had been mounting in her head over the past months" (128). Derek's ideology has developed since attending New College. He now believes in the Holocaust, to some degree; he doesn't use racial slurs; he now likes and accepts Jews, even considers them white; he no longer considers himself "a white supremacist, because he no longer believed whites were necessarily better than other people. He was simply a white nationalist, which meant he thought whites needed to be protected within their own border, like an endangered species" (129). However, he is still against mixed-race marriage and biracial children; he still believes white Europeans have higher IQ scores than other races; he still believes black men have higher levels of testosterone, which he believes leads to "a greater propensity for violence" (129); he still believes in the threat of white genocide. Allison is hopeful because Derek "based his prejudice not on an intractable gut feeling but on what he thought to be a logical theory" (129). There is a possibility that she can dismantle his logic and show him scientifically that his theories are incorrect.

Allison and Derek debate throughout the summer, sometimes all day. They have bitter disagreements and some arguments end in tears, but the debates persist. By the end of the summer, Derek has softened his beliefs further, but has not abandoned them. He shows his confusion in the convoluted explanations and rationalizations he offers to maintain his white nationalist identity while ceding the ideology's underlying rationale. He still will not abandon his claims of white genocide. He invites Allison to attend his second annual *Stormfront* conference.

Chapters 4-6 Analysis

Matthew's strategy is to force Derek to confront his own internal conflict about white nationalism by showing Derek his own humanity. Matthew believes that if he debates Derek, Derek will only dig in further to his white nationalist beliefs. Derek responds well to Matthew's approach. He is lonely on a campus that despises him, and his desire for social engagement leads Derek to engage in a social setting he would have otherwise avoided. Matthew's friends and others on campus debate the effectiveness of this approach, but it works. Derek becomes friends with people he previously saw as enemies; ideology that he once viewed in the abstract now has real consequences to people he cares about; he grows to respect them, their intelligence, and their opinions, and consequently wonders if so many intelligent people whom he respects could be wrong about his ideology.

Much of Derek's conflict results from his family's roots in white nationalism. White nationalism isn't just something his father believes in—it is the foundation of his parents' relationship and their social network. Don has been to federal prison because of white nationalism; Derek's family structured their entire life and Derek's upbringing around white nationalism. Abandoning white nationalist ideology is akin to Derek abandoning his family.

As he softens in his white nationalist ideology, Allison's direct confrontation of Derek's beliefs accelerates the progress. Matthew's nonconfrontational approach was valuable in making Derek receptive to such arguments, but he needs someone to directly confront him the way Allison does to fully address the flaws in his ideology and abandon it altogether. This process is difficult for both Allison and Derek, but it is necessary to overcome Derek's years of indoctrination.

Chapters 7-9

Chapter 7 Summary: "This Is Scary"

Allison agrees to attend Derek's *Stormfront* conference because she believes Derek is being dishonest with her about his beliefs, "watering down the true extent of his racism in order to preserve their friendship" (140). She wants to know if his arguments change in tone or substance when he is with his white supremacist followers. Allison also believes that by attending the conference, she will show Derek she is making a sincere effort to understand his beliefs, allowing her to earn his trust, then build a case against white nationalism.

The recent presidential election energizes the conference. Racial dog whistles dominate the Republican party's talking points and after the election racial hate crimes surge to historic levels. Conference attendees believe the country has reached a racial tipping point that will trigger the white supremacist revolution they have been waiting for. To Allison's surprise, Derek's family is kind and welcoming. Their discussion topics are odd: gripes about "brown people," Obama, Jews, and political correctness, but they are otherwise pleasant and loving people. At the conference, Allison notices, "Where she had expected to find only bigotry and nastiness, she also recognized something else" (149). She tells Derek, "These people genuinely love and adore you" (149). Derek concludes the conference with his keynote speech. Saslow notes, "After months of conversations with Allison, he was slowly becoming less secure in his beliefs. Whereas before he had catered his message exclusively to white nationalists, he now was at least aware of another perspective" (151). Derek's speech avoids potentially hurtful topics and instead focuses solely on the demographic decline of whites in America. The conference shows Allison that Derek is more central to the white nationalist movement than she previously realized.

Chapter 8 Summary: "Another Debate, and Another Midnight"

After Derek's *Stormfront* conference, Allison feels "more prepared than ever to begin debating Derek in earnest" (162). She enrolls in a course on prejudice and employs lessons from her curriculum in debate with Derek. Saslow says, "Each Monday and Thursday, there was Allison [...] taking notes about their discussions on psychological science to arm herself for the next conversation with Derek" (163). Allison periodically injects white nationalism into conversations, hoping to influence Derek's opinions. She sends him scientific studies refuting his long-held beliefs: articles showing race is a fluid and unscientific concept; articles refuting Derek's beliefs on race and IQ; articles illustrating white privilege over other races in contemporary United States. Allison also brings emotion into Derek's scientific debates to illustrate to him the real, actual harm these ideas inflict on people. Saslow elaborates, "Allison repeatedly pushed their conversations from theoretical to intimate, hoping to make Derek confront the reality of his beliefs" (168). As they debate, their relationship transitions from friendship to romantic.

Don notices a change in Derek's behavior. Derek insists that his beliefs are unchanged, but he stops posting on *Stormfront* and tempers his on-air rhetoric. He begins skipping his radio show to paddle on his kayak and think. Derek ponders his beliefs and future. Saslow elaborates, "Derek's brain was also crowded with new ideas, backed by data and dozens of studies, which suggested white nationalism was both dangerous and flawed" (175). The ideas Derek once subscribed to now seem to him cruel and wrong. Around Thanksgiving of 2012, instigated by a post about him on the New College forum, Derek finally responds publicly to his critics and tentatively embraces his new mindset. Derek writes, in part:

> I do not and would never support discrimination or unfair treatment against anyone insofar as my privilege allows me to identify it. I am not a white supremacist, nor do I identify with white supremacy. I don't hate anyone because of race, religion, or anything similar. I am not a Nazi, nor do I identify with Nazism. I am not part of the KKK, nor do I identify with the KKK. As far as Stormfront goes, it's my dad's website, and though I have moderator privileges, I don't moderate. And as should be understood for both the radio and the website, only things I've said myself are things I can be held accountable for (184).

This equivocal renunciation of Derek's beliefs satiates the student body, but something still concerns Allison: the SPLC maintains a public "extremist file" on Derek. Allison forwards Derek's forum post to the organization, hoping it will convince them to remove him from their website.

Instead, the center contacts Derek for comment before publishing his full post.

Chapter 9 Summary: "I'm Torn"

Derek responds to the SPLC, "My forum post and my racial ideology are not mutually exclusive concepts [...] Everything I said is true, and I also believe in White Nationalism" (190-91). The truth is more complicated. Derek is contemplating a life free of white nationalism, as an academic in a quiet college town. He is increasingly abandoning elements of his ideology, but is bound to it through his family, for whom "white nationalism wasn't just a belief system; it was the glue that held together friendships and family" (190). Rejecting the label white nationalism is rejecting Derek's family and friends, and is the most difficult part of his transformation.

Derek loses any progress he made with his classmates at New College when they read his response to the SPLC article. The community shuns him. He wonders if white nationalism is worth such exclusion and if his classmates "were valid in their criticism and righteous in their anger [...] if white nationalism was inherently flawed and morally indefensible" (197). He researches and finds flawed many of his prior conceptions about whiteness in medieval Europe and other aspects of human history. He researches statistics on race in America and learns that many of his beliefs on white genocide are also flawed. He becomes "increasingly convinced that the structures of white supremacy remained very much in place" (202). By 2013, he says to Allison of white nationalism, "The ideology is flawed, and I've moved away from it" (203).

Chapters 7-9 Analysis

While Derek is relinquishing his white nationalist ideology, due to Derek's advocacy it is increasingly becoming accepted in mainstream America. Allison has become Derek's most fervent adversary and is also his closest friend. By attending Derek's *Stormfront* conference and continuing to engage with him on the subject, she persistently erodes the foundations of Derek's beliefs. Allison adjusts her college curriculum to better debate Derek and continues pushing him on the subject even when it is painful and seems hopeless. She begins presenting Derek scientific studies refuting what he previously accepted as truth. Everything—emotion, logic, science— overwhelms Derek's tortured intellect and leads him to conclude his white supremacist ideology is flawed. He issues a public partial rejection of white supremacism, but familial bonds prevent him from fully denouncing white nationalism. Derek has settled his internal conflict and renounced white nationalism as a personal ideology, but he struggles with any public renunciation or condemnation because he knows it will destroy his relationship with his family and community of white nationalists.

Chapters 10-11

Chapter 10 Summary: "I Have to Do This Now"

In his final months of college, Derek's only goal is to avoid controversy and appease both his classmates and his family—"To somehow recede from the front lines of white nationalism so quietly that no one would notice or care" (204). Western Michigan University accepts him into their graduate program on medieval studies. He wants an easy resolution to this conflict. Allison pushes him to publicly denounce white nationalism, reminding him of the "public archive" of ideas Derek built during his time at the forefront of the movement. By now, members of the Republican party have absorbed Derek's lessons on moving white nationalism to the mainstream. The Tea Party and Republican politicians like Jeff Sessions and Steve King parrot Derek's talking points and use racial dog whistles to bring white nationalist policies to the forefront of American politics. Allison tells him, "You have an obligation to say in public that you don't believe in this, and that you were factually and morally wrong" (206).

Derek wants to skip his graduation ceremony, but it is important to his family. His mother and grandmother attend, but Don stays home because his attendance would be too controversial. Don still believes that Derek is a committed white nationalist and that Derek's degree will enable the white nationalist movement to advance. Derek receives his diploma and the event concludes with little incident.

Allison convinces Derek that for the sake of his own future, he must publicly denounce white nationalism. She convinces Derek that if a public record exists of his white nationalist views, he will never escape those views in his academic, professional, or personal life. Derek agrees, but wants to tell his parents before he makes a public statement. He visits his parents the day after a jury acquits George Zimmerman in his shooting of Trayvon Martin. As he listens to his father discuss the case, his confusion about his father's views turns to anger. Derek realizes, "It wasn't just his father's views that suddenly horrified him […] It was the memory of his previous self" (217). He made those same arguments and "expressed similar callousness, ignorance, and cruelty" (217). He cannot muster the courage to discuss his new viewpoint with his parents in person. He leaves his parents' house and drafts a full denunciation of his white nationalist beliefs and his past, then sends it to the Southern Poverty Law Center with the instruction, "Please publish in full" (220).

Chapter 11 Summary: "So Much Worse Than I Ever Thought"

While performing an internet search of Derek to track his rise as a public figure, Don finds the headline, "Activist Son of Key Racist Leader Renounces White Nationalism" (221). The full text of the article is Derek's letter—an evisceration of white nationalist ideology that references structural oppression, privilege, and marginalized groups. Don assumes the article is fake and calls Derek to warn him someone hacked his email. Derek tells Don the letter is authentic and Don abruptly hangs up. Saslow recounts, "The next hours unfolded in a cycle of rage and grief" (222). Don, Chloe, or another member of his family call Derek in rage, hang up, call back later to apologize, then repeat. Don believes two things: (1) white nationalism is a righteous cause; (2) Derek is one of the most intelligent people he knows. Those two beliefs are now in conflict. Don tells Derek this is "by far the worst experience of his life" and that he "weighed out the pros and cons, and he had concluded that it would have been better for their family if Derek hadn't been born" (223). Moments later, Don calls back and tells Derek that isn't true and apologizes. Derek confides in Allison, "I think I might be getting disowned. Many family members have vowed never to talk to me again […] it's so much worse than I ever thought" (224).

Derek receives a different reaction from outside his family. He receives congratulatory messages from friends, former classmates, and strangers supportive of his ideological evolution. The Southern Poverty Law Center removes

Derek's extremist file from its website. Derek publicly credits the influence of New College students for his transformation, especially those who disagreed with his ideology but supported him regardless. He says:

> Furthermore, a critical juncture was when I'd realize that a friend was considered an outsider by the philosophy I supported. It's a huge contradiction to share your summer plans with someone whom you completely respect, only to then realize that your ideology doesn't consider them a full member of society. I couldn't resolve that (225).

Stormfront users call Derek a traitor, threaten him, and question Don's allegiance to their cause. Duke believes Derek is suffering a form of Stockholm syndrome from liberal academia. Don contemplates withdrawing from public life.

Unwelcome in his childhood home, Derek meets Don in a bar before leaving Florida for Michigan. They debate, but it is fruitless. Weeks later, Derek returns to Florida to legally change his name from Derek Roland Black to Roland Derek Black. It is a minor change that he believes will hide him from search engine results referencing his past. He doesn't see his family while he's back. He tells Allison, "It's all over and done with" (235), but at the same time, the white nationalist conference he founded is promoting and spreading the ideas Derek pioneered.

Chapters 10-11 Analysis

Derek has fully renounced white nationalism privately, but cannot bring himself to do so publicly. As the 2016 presidential election approaches, mainstream politicians begin adopting the racialized language Derek championed for in his white nationalist lectures. As white nationalism becomes more mainstream, he feels responsible for the ideology's spread and culpable for atrocities committed in its name. Encouraged by Allison, he feels increasing pressure to condemn the ideology. When Derek finally publicly denounces white nationalism, he does so without warning his parents. His betrayal to their core values shocks them. Their initial reaction is severe, but even after the shock subsides, they choose white nationalist ideology over their son. They effectively disown Derek, telling him he is no longer welcome in their home. In the next few years, Derek rarely sees or speaks to them. When he does, it is combative—never familial. Derek's worst fear in renouncing white nationalist ideology is realized—it ruins his relationship with his family and entire network of friends built prior to enrolling in college. He sacrifices almost everything in his life to do what he believes is morally righteous.

Chapters 12-14

Chapter 12 Summary: "Primed for This Revolution"

At the now renamed Derek Black Memorial Conference, Don and Duke discuss the power the internet has given them to recruit white supremacists and spread their ideology globally. Don says of the internet, "[W]e can get our own message out now" (237). They notice the spread of their movement into the mainstream, adopted by politicians across the country, giving them "covert allies in surprising places" (238). The crowd at the conference is also "younger than ever before" (239), filled with "disaffected young men." One such disaffected young man is Spencer, "a PhD student who left Duke University to launch a popular blog called *Alternative Right*" (239).

Derek is in Michigan trying to move on from his prior life. He concluded that white nationalism is wrong, but two decades of conditioning "hardwired it into every part of his subconscious" (240). He is learning to trust the government, exposing himself to popular culture and music for the first time, and "retraining his brain." He couch surfs to meet new people and engage with multicultural America; he and Allison travel to immerse themselves in foreign cultures; he never, as a personal rule, discusses white nationalism. Out of fear, he shares his address only with Allison and his parents. Don often messages Derek with provocations, which he ignores.

The Black Lives Matter movement is now prominent. Don believes the protests are evidence of a looming race war. Derek now finds himself on the side of the minority protestors. Allison is his only confidant during his period of personal growth, "the bridge between Derek and Roland" (245). *Stormfront* radicalizes Dylann Roof, and he murders nine members of the congregation at a historically black church in an attempt to start a race war. Derek wonders if his old speeches or radio shows helped radicalize Dylann. When Donald Trump announces his candidacy in a racially charged speech that to Derek harkens to Ku Klux Klan messaging, Derek sees the product of his white nationalist messaging lectures coming to fruition—but he is now fearful rather than optimistic. To combat the growing popularity of an ideology he formerly espoused, he begins sharing his story publicly. It feels hopeless though. Derek laments, "Nothing I can say will undo the damage" (259).

Chapter 13 Summary: "All-Out Mayhem"

Donald Trump's presidential election victory makes white nationalists feel like they won the country's biggest popularity contest. Trump encourages white nationalists by staffing his administration with people they believe are sympathetic to their ideology: General Michael Flynn, Senator Jeff Sessions, Stephen Miller, Julie Kirchner, and Steve Bannon. Spencer is becoming a rising star of the "alt-right," a rebranding term applied to young white supremacists. Spencer states at a press conference, "The alt-right is obviously real, and it's obviously growing" (263). Don admires Spencer's polish. He believes Spencer is becoming what Duke strove to be throughout his political career and what Derek could have been. Saslow explains, "If white nationalism was going to transition into a viable political movement, it needed leaders with mainstream credentials, and Spencer checked every box" (263-64).

Derek publishes an opinion piece in *The New York Times* in response to the rise of the "alt-right" and mainstream acceptance of white nationalism. It states in part, "More and more people are being forced to recognize now what I learned early: Our country is susceptible to some of our worst instincts when the message is packaged correctly" (267). *Stormfront* members discuss the story on the site's message boards, driving a further wedge between Derek and his family. Derek no longer sees his family and rarely speaks with them on the phone. Without Derek involved in *Stormfront*, Don is lonely and joyless. Derek begins to speak at colleges on the dangers of white nationalism and Don labels him an anti-white activist in opposition to his family's work. Don begins working more closely with Spencer, who has moved to Arlington, Virginia to build his brand of white nationalism. Don is an informal advisor to Spencer, leading him on the path he previously believed was Derek's destiny. Derek is trying "to build some kind of a bridge—a way to communicate with his father that didn't have to involve politics or Richard Spencer" (275).

Chapter 14 Summary: "We Were Wrong"

Derek returns home for the first time in over a year. His goal is to reunite and form some relationship with his family independent of white nationalism. Don won't stop teasing Derek "with little jabs;" Chloe insists on watching the entire Fox News nightly line-up of shows, then rewatching Tucker Carlson's show because he is "Don and Chloe's favorite and a new hero among the alt-right" (278); Derek ignores their instigations and festers, wishing he could find some opening to reform their relationship. Don attempts to convince Derek to return to his radio show. Derek explains to Don, "I was wrong [...] *We* were wrong" (281).

In the ensuing months, white nationalism explodes into mainstream politics: the battle over destruction of Confederate monuments, a flurry of white nationalist marches and rallies, and more murders. Don and Derek become more entrenched in their beliefs and advocate more strongly for their now opposing causes. Their divide is now unbridgeable. Don argues to Derek, "Everything you advocated for is finally beginning to catch on [...] Don't you see that?" (283). Derek responds, "Of course [...] We're coming up to the critical moment. That's why I'm trying to warn people" (283).

Chapters 12-14 Analysis

Derek's life is now opposite of his former life. He fully engages with the world and embraces multiculturalism. He is now a stranger to his family, who no longer recognizes the man their child has become. As the Black Lives Matter movement grows alongside a surge in white nationalism, Derek rises in opposition to Don, Duke, and his former white nationalist community. Don and Duke work with "alt-right" firebrands like Spencer and Milo Yiannopoulos to continue Derek's work in bringing white nationalism into mainstream acceptance. Derek speaks publicly and pens op-eds in major publications exposing the evils of his family's ideology and publicly denouncing it. Derek hoped he could abandon his family's ideology and alter their relationship into a positive nonpolitical one, but that did not happen. Derek's intellect, when exposed to the broader world, has grown beyond the confines in which they tried to cage it through years of homeschooling and indoctrination. Derek's relationship to his family was always structured around his utility as a white nationalist rather than typical familial bonds. Now that he has abandoned the ideology and begun to actively oppose it, his relationship to his family is that of an enemy which they must defeat.

Derek Black

Derek is the son of former Ku Klux Klan Grand Wizard and *Stormfront* online hate group creator, Don Black, and the godson on former Ku Klux Klan Grand Wizard, white supremacist politician, and notorious public figure, David Duke. Derek is homeschooled and indoctrinated with white nationalist ideology. He becomes a rising star in the white nationalist movement. After attending college, he publicly renounces white nationalism and denounces the ideology. He currently speaks and writes publicly against white nationalism in the United States.

Don Black

Don is Derek's father and radio show cohost. Don became involved in the white supremacist movement as a teenager. He later became the Grand Wizard of the Ku Klux Klan and founded *Stormfront*, an online hate group for white supremacists. Don is Chloe's husband.

Chloe Black

Chloe is Derek's mother. She shares a white supremacist ideology but is not as active as Derek or Don in the movement. Chloe is Don's wife.

David Duke

Duke is a world-famous white supremacist. He is a former Grand Wizard of the Ku Klux Klan and a politician. He is unwelcome in several countries because of his outspoken beliefs. He was married to Chloe before Don. Duke is Derek's godfather and mentor.

Juan Elias

Juan is Derek's first friend at New College. He is a Peruvian immigrant from Miami. Juan is friends with Derek during his tenure at New College, even after a classmate exposes Derek as a white nationalist.

Matthew Stevenson

Matthew is an Orthodox Jewish student at New College who befriends Derek and invites him to his weekly Shabbat dinners after a classmate exposes Derek as a white nationalist. Matthew concocts the plan to convince Derek to renounce his white nationalist ideology through nonjudgmental inclusion.

Rose

Rose is a Jewish New College student from Arkansas. Rose and Derek's relationship begins as friendship and turns romantic. Derek's relationship with Rose begins to make him question his ideology that labels Jews as an enemy. After a classmate exposes Derek's white nationalism, Rose ceases communication with Derek.

Allison Gornik

Allison is Matthew's roommate and eventually becomes Derek's girlfriend. Allison is a psychology major at New College. She is from Ohio. She is fascinated by people and is a skilled debater. Over several years, Allison and several classmates convince Derek to abandon and publicly renounce white nationalist ideology.

Donald Trump

Trump is the 45th President of the United States of America. He is a former businessman and public figure. He developed a following among white nationalists by publicly attacking President Barack Obama as being a Kenyan Muslim rather than an American citizen. He was later elected to the presidency with the support of the white nationalist community in a campaign many describe as racially charged.

Richard Spencer

Spencer is a leader in the "alt-right," a rebranding of the white nationalist movement. He is a public figure pushing white nationalism into mainstream politics with the help of Don and Duke.

White Nationalism/White Supremacy

White nationalism is an umbrella term for an ideology espousing white supremacist or white separatist ideologies, often alleging inferiority of nonwhites. Derek's ideological transformation provides Saslow an opportunity to explore white nationalism in all its iterations, from the violent felonious activity of Don attempting to overthrow a peaceful island nation to form a whites-only mecca to the more innocuous forms of white separatism that do not allege superiority, but rather advocate for a more harmonious existence through racial separation. Saslow is also able to illustrate through Derek, Don, Duke, and others the connection between seemingly benign forms of white nationalism and violent ones, showing that they are part of the same harmful ideology and often work in concert.

Mainstream Acceptance of White Nationalism

Derek's major contribution to the white nationalist movement is to adjust its semantics to make it approachable in the mainstream and acceptable for politicians to espouse. Derek does this through manipulation of the language and presentation. Derek successfully distances white nationalism from the Ku Klux Klan and historical violence and reframes it as something acceptable for mainstream white America. This process begins before Derek, with the efforts of Don and Duke, but Derek's construction of a children's white nationalism game, lectures on language, and personal actions in politics and on his radio show lead the movement to a new level of acceptance in United States politics and society.

Internal Conflict

Derek is conflicted internally throughout Saslow's book. As he is continually exposed to new perspectives, cultures, and scientific research, his internal conflict with the indoctrination he received in his youth grows. Derek is intelligent enough to feel that his ideology is wrong, but it takes years of internal debate to arrive at the conclusions he needs to renounce white nationalism.

Nonjudgmental Inclusion

Derek's friends practice nonjudgmental inclusion throughout Derek's transformation to subtly guide him away from white nationalism without directly confronting him on the topic. Derek's racial and religious minority friends continue engaging with him socially because they believe he will acknowledge their humanity, and such acknowledgement will lead him to recognize them as equals and abandon white supremacist beliefs. They interact with Derek in ways distanced from white nationalism and ignore the ideology altogether.

Family

Family is at the heart of Derek's story. Derek's family isolates and indoctrinates him with white nationalist ideology. The white nationalist community acts as Derek's second family. They provide his intellectual roots and his sense of belonging. When he undergoes his intellectual transformation and abandons white nationalism, it is his college family who guides his transformation. His college family supports him when his biological family abandons him. After Derek's beliefs are exposed on campus, his friends embrace him as family, refusing to abandon him even though he espouses an ideology hurtful to them—

putting in the time to cure someone they've come to love, regardless of how painful the process may be. Whether it is Derek's biological family who indoctrinated him with a hateful ideology or his college family who struggled with him to overcome such hate, family is central to Derek's journey.

Dog Whistle

A form of political messaging in which coded language is employed that appears to mean one thing but has another meaning to a subgroup. Dog whistles are often employed by politicians signaling to white supremacists that policies will have racial effects, without explicitly stating racist intent.

Ku Klux Klan

The Ku Klux Klan is a white supremacist hate group that targets African Americans. The Klan is a reactionary white nationalist group that is anti-immigrant, anti-Catholic, and anti-Jewish, among other groups.

Privilege

Privilege is a special right, advantage, or immunity granted to a person or group. In this context, the relevant privilege is "white privilege." White privilege is the societal privilege of white people over nonwhite people.

Stormfront

Stormfront is a white nationalist internet forum and the first major racial hate site.

White Genocide

White genocide is a conspiracy theory that a deliberate plot exists to cause the extinction of whites through miscegenation, mass immigration, racial integration, low fertility rates, abortion, governmental land-confiscation, organized violence, and forced assimilation. Theorists often blame Jews, blacks, Hispanics, and Muslims.

1. "No family had done more to help white nationalism bully its way back into mainstream politics, and Derek was the next step in that evolution. He was precocious, thoughtful, and polite, sometimes delivering handwritten thank-you notes to conference volunteers. He never used racist slurs. He didn't advocate for outright violence or breaking the law. His core beliefs were the same as those of most white nationalists that America would be better off as a whites-only country, and that all minorities should eventually be forced to leave. […] His goal, he explained once on the radio, was to 'normalize these white nationalist ideas that already fit so neatly within the divides of modern society." (Chapter 1, Pages 7-8)

   Derek's major contribution to white nationalism is to make the movement acceptable in mainstream white culture. He does this by reforming the language and presentation of white nationalism while maintaining the same ideals that existed in earlier iterations of white nationalism. Derek makes the movement a wolf in sheep's clothing.

2. "New College was more than 80 percent white, but it was also listed in college guides as the most liberal school in Florida, the best school for hippies, the most gay-friendly, the most pot-friendly, the most likely to 'transform your life and your worldview.' One day on their radio show, as Derek readied to leave for a four-year college, a caller asked Don if he was worried about his son moving away from home to live 'among the enemy in a hotbed of multiculturalism.' Don started to laugh. 'Derek's the original nonconformist,' he said. 'It's not like any of these little commies are going to

impact his thinking. If anyone is going to be influenced here, it will be them.'" (Chapter 1, Page 23)

Derek's decision to attend a politically progressive school is questionable, given his white supremacist ideology. Both Derek and Don are confident that Derek's intellect and commitment to white supremacism are strong enough to withstand influence from his progressive professors and classmates.

3. "In the mornings while [Derek's] classmates slept, he walked alone to a patch of grass outside the dorm and called in to his [political radio] show to join his father on the air, and together they railed against the minority takeover. Whenever his classmates asked, Derek explained his morning ritual as a daily catch-up call with his unusually close family. Then he hung up the phone, returned to the center of campus, and befriended whoever walked by." (Chapter 2, Page 29)

Derek leads a dual life that creates internal conflict. Derek spends his early mornings discussing white nationalism on his radio show, then meets his college friends and behaves in a progressive, accepting manner so naturally that no one suspects he could harbor an ideology considered hateful.

4. "What Rose didn't know was that Derek was constantly trying to quiet his own feelings and telling himself to back away. His two most serious former girlfriends had both been committed white nationalists, a daughter and a granddaughter of major leaders within the movement, people whose beliefs mirrored his own. It was one thing to befriend an outsider; his father and David Duke had both done plenty of that, and sometimes it could even be useful. But dating a Jew felt to Derek like a double

betrayal-first and foremost of his own beliefs, and then also of Rose, who had no idea about his history or his racial convictions." (Chapter 2, Page 35)

New College has a profound impact on Derek from the outset. It is not the college itself that begins to erode Derek's ideology, but his fellow classmates. Don and Chloe sheltered Derek his entire life. His entire social network prior to New College is white nationalist, so New College exposes him to diverse groups of people for the first time. As he meets more people, Derek realizes he likes them and they are nothing like the stereotypes presented to him by white nationalists. This realization is the first step in Derek shedding his ideology.

5. "But what became most evident at New College during those first overnight hours was the beginnings of an ideological rift, a divide that would widen over the next few years on campus. Ultimately, similar debates at campuses all over the country would convulse, splitting America's liberal Left. What was the appropriate response to the most intolerant kinds of free speech? Exclusion or inclusion? Was it better to shame and demonize Derek? Or was it more effective to somehow reach out to him?" (Chapter 3, Pages 49-50)

Derek's story exists in a larger narrative than that of personal transformation. In the coming years, "Dereks" would pop up all over the country, and the country would engage in a debate of how to address hate in its communities. Colleges implement a variety of policies—some intended to ensure student safety, some in response to student concerns. College students band together in opposition to hate speech, some peaceful and some violent. This debate, which has reached cable news and even the desk of the President of the United States, persists.

6. "[Derek] wasn't a white supremacist, he said, but in fact a white nationalist—or, better yet, a racial egalitarian. He told [Rose] that he believed all races were in fact equal but that whites were better served living apart from other races. He told her words like 'racist' had been invented to demonize well-meaning white people. He said races had inherent biological differences, and for evidence he cited discredited studies based on flawed data that showed a small average differential in IQ scores between whites and blacks. He said the cornerstone of his belief was fear of a white genocide, and for proof he showed her recent census data that indicated the rising minority population in the United States." (Chapter 3, Page 54)

   Derek is beginning to soften his racial ideology. He no longer believes whites are superior to other races but maintains the ideology of white separatism, believes in the conspiracy theory of white genocide, and adheres to debunked pseudoscience on racial IQ differentials. Derek's process of abandoning white nationalist ideology is gradual and that requires persistent attack from his friends.

7. "'There is no better way to make sure Derek keeps these abhorrent views than if we all exclude him,' Matthew said. But nonjudgmental inclusion—Matthew believed that tactic had potential, and the more he researched Derek, the more convinced he became. On Stormfront, Matthew learned Derek had been homeschooled by his white nationalist family and therefore spent little time with people of color or Jews. [...] Matthew began working to build a relationship in

which Derek might be able to learn what the enemy was actually like. 'The goal was really just to make Jews more human for him,' Matthew said." (Chapter 4, Page 81)

Matthew's belief that nonjudgmental inclusion will lead to Derek abandoning his white nationalist beliefs is based on thorough research of Derek's past. Matthew learns that Derek's parents sheltered him from nonwhite, non-European cultures and infers that his view of such cultures is based entirely on propaganda. This is reminiscent of Germany during the Holocaust. Most Germans had never seen a real Jew and were familiar only with a propagandized version designed to elicit fear and hatred. Matthew reasons that by befriending Derek, he and Juan can convey their humanity to him and that will lead to Derek renouncing white nationalism independently.

8. "When some of Matthew's other friends privately denigrated Derek's character, calling him a racist and an oppressor, Matthew insisted on treating Derek with respect, even compassion. 'In some ways, he just has way bigger versions of the same hang-ups we all have,' Matthew told a friend once. He believed it was human nature to separate into groups, to define oneself against the other. [...] Everyone had prejudices, Matthew thought, even if Derek's were much more extreme and pronounced." (Chapter 4, Pages 95-96)

Matthew's empathy allows him to engage in the nonjudgmental inclusion that leads to Derek's ideological transformation. Matthew views Derek from an unemotional, nonjudgmental perspective, reasoning that less pronounced versions of Derek's hang-ups exist in everyone.

9. "Whatever his classmates might have mistaken as the first hints of softening—Derek's civility, his intellectual curiosity—were the exact characteristics that made Don more certain than ever about his son's potential as a white nationalist leader. Every slur Derek never said, every enemy he never made, every minority he somehow managed to befriend, was all more proof of what Don already believed: Only someone like Derek could lead white nationalism beyond its violent history of swastikas and white robes and into the multicultural mainstream of twenty-first-century politics." (Chapter 5, Page 98)

   The same characteristics that Don and Duke praise in Derek, that they believe make him a valuable tool in white nationalism, are the characteristics that lead Derek to renounce his beliefs. He treats everyone with respect, befriends people of many cultures, and accepts and welcomes everyone for who they are. To Don, these are signs that Derek can be a polished, socially acceptable face for white nationalism, but to an outside observer, these are signs that Derek is not truly committed to such a hateful ideology.

10. "And Don would go quietly back to Alabama, back to the library, back to the same worn copy of *Our Nordic Race*. He lacked the ego and the confidence to be a political demagogue like Duke. He didn't believe in sparking a revolution through violence, murder, or detonating bombs like Franklin. But in the pages of *Our Nordic Race*, Don found the outlines of another kind of racial soldier. 'A problem to be solved by the cold process of intellect,' the book had instructed, and that was the kind of leadership Don hoped to provide." (Chapter 5, Page 106)

Don is the technician of white nationalism. In Don's prime, Duke was the political face of the movement, Franklin was the praxis, and Don was the intellectual technician. Don works behind the scenes to enable the public-facing and action-oriented white nationalists to achieve their ends.

11. "Why, instead of confronting this infamous white nationalist and challenging his beliefs, was she making his campus life more pleasant and comfortable? [...] She liked him. She trusted him. She was attracted to him. She felt increasingly convinced that he was inherently different from the overt racists whose hateful messages she read on Stormfront. And yet she was in no way willing to let their relationship become romantic. That would be tantamount to aligning herself on campus with Derek and all he'd chosen to represent." (Chapter 6, Page 125)

Befriending Derek makes campus life difficult. It also incites internal conflict within the students befriending Derek, who question the effectiveness of their strategy. Everyone who befriends Derek and practices nonjudgmental inclusion at some point wonders if they are enabling him or if he is persuading them to his own ideology rather than him to theirs. Derek makes this more difficult for his friends by being a likeable person. Allison is falling for Derek but can't bring herself to act on romantic feelings because of Derek's white nationalist ideology.

12. "In 2012 the Republican Party had essentially decided to forfeit the minority vote. It had chosen, as Derek once predicted, to become an overwhelmingly white party, and now the decisive question of the election was

whether enough white voters remained." (Chapter 7, Page 141)

Derek's white nationalist revolution is coming to fruition. In 2012, the ideology is gaining mainstream acceptance and major politicians are adopting it. After President Obama wins a second term, racial tensions among the populace explode. The Republican Party embraces disaffected white voters and becomes the de facto political party of white nationalists in the United States. It does so by employing Derek's techniques of employing white nationalism as subtext without explicitly espousing anything hateful.

13. "Most of all, she thought the best way to make an effective argument against Derek's beliefs was to first make a legitimate effort to fully understand them. Only that way could she earn his complete trust. Only then could she build a case against white nationalism using not just her values but also his values and his vocabulary. By going to the conference, she would earn her way into those conversations. Maybe one of those conversations would trigger a shift." (Chapter 7, Page 142)

Allison takes a risk in attending Derek's Stormfront conference. She believes she needs to go all-in to save Derek from this ideology. Allison loves Derek and is willing to do anything necessary to save him from what she perceives as a psychological illness plaguing him, even if the process harms her.

14. "But now Derek was almost twenty-three, an adult who had been living apart from his parents for a few years, and he was still just as devoted to spreading their ideology. Moshe worried: What if all he had done by

befriending Derek was to enable him, to provide him with cover from the social justice activists on campus so that he could continue to promote a racist ideology while living a comfortable college life?" (Chapter 7, Page 160)

The slow process of grinding away Derek's ideology is exhausting for his friends and sometimes feels hopeless. After several years of Shabbat dinners, nonjudgmental inclusion, and debates, it seems like Derek is no closer to abandoning white nationalism. Engaging with Derek has been an arduous and painful process for his friends, one which has made their campus life difficult.

15. "But sometimes Allison wanted their conversations about race to be emotionally charged. White nationalism wasn't just some academic thought experiment. It was a caustic, harmful ideology that was causing real damage to people's lives, so Allison began to send Derek links about that, too." (Chapter 8, Page 168)

Allison begins to stray from nonjudgmental inclusion. Derek grounds his beliefs in logic and reason. He is a prominent white nationalist because he removes emotion from his ideology. Allison wants to inject emotion into Derek's ideology by connecting it to his friends and illustrating to him the real impacts it has on their lives. This is the most confrontational that Derek's New College friends have been to his beliefs, but it is also a necessary step to Derek's ideological transformation.

16. "After poring over so many of Allison's psychological studies, Derek no longer believed the white nationalist myths he had propagated about 'Jewish manipulation,'

'testosterone-fueled black aggression,' or larger brain sizes for whites. He was becoming unsure that his theory about IQ discrepancies held up to the best modern science. During his time at New College, Derek had gone from believing whites were a superior race in need of an exclusive homeland, to thinking all races were equal but should be preserved by living separately, to thinking that segregation wasn't really necessary so long as whites weren't forced to assimilate." (Chapter 8, Page 182)

Derek has now abandoned the core of his white nationalist beliefs. He no longer believes in white supremacism, white separatism, or faulty IQ science. He now has many friends who are racial and religious minorities, and he no longer believes much of what white nationalists believe, but he won't abandon the moniker because of his strong familial and social connection to white nationalism. His roots are tied-up in the ideology, and even if he reasons that the ideology is flawed, the label is difficult for him to untangle from.

17. "In their online chats, Derek had begun to imagine the possibilities of an anonymous life removed from white nationalism: earning a PhD, teaching at a university, and raising a family in a quiet college town." (Chapter 9, Page 188)

Derek no longer wants to be a white nationalist, especially not publicly. He wants more than anything to reinvent his life and pursue his academic goals without the movement hanging over him.

18. "Derek forwarded the SPLC story to Allison in Australia. She was disappointed he had publicly reaffirmed his commitment to white nationalism, but

she also knew that for Derek rejecting that label was likely to be the last and most difficult part of any transformation, because the identity was so central to his family connections. She believed his evolution was still under way, and she understood the inherent pressure he felt from his parents and Duke." (Chapter 9, Page 191)

Much of Derek's commitment to white nationalism is rooted in his familial and social relationships. This has been the case since his indoctrination: He grew within the movement while attending conferences with Don, spending quality time and forming childhood memories with his father; a large part of his schooling was spent building the Stormfront kids website alongside his father; when he travels, he crashes with other white nationalists. The white nationalist community has been a part of Derek's life since he was born—the most infamous white nationalist, Duke, is Derek's godfather. He wants to renounce the ideology but doing so means upending his entire life.

19. "He also could no longer quiet another alarm that had begun to go off with increasing frequency inside his head: What if so many of his classmates on the forum were valid in their criticism and righteous in their anger? What if white nationalism was inherently flawed and morally indefensible? It had been easy to dismiss their forum posts when he felt convinced of his beliefs, but now his certainty had shrunk down into something he could no longer define." (Chapter 9, Page 197)

Matthew's nonjudgmental inclusion is beginning to show results. Derek is now part of a community of diverse minds whose intellect he respects. This creates a problem for Derek: When "the enemy" was abstract and unknown, Derek could easily write off their anger, but now those angry with him are friends whom he respects. He can no longer ignore their hurt and anger; it must be justified.

20. "As he traveled through Europe, Derek read historical texts from the eighth to the twelfth century, trying to trace back the modern concepts of race and whiteness, but he couldn't find them anywhere. Instead, the facts of history pointed him to another conclusion: The iconic European warriors so often celebrated on Stormfront had never thought of themselves as white, Derek decided. Some of them had considered skin color not a hard biological fact but a condition that could change over time based on culture, diet, and climate. They had fought not for their race but for religion, culture, power, and money, just like every other empire of the Middle Ages." (Chapter 9, Pages 201-2)

Every step forward Derek makes is the combination of emotion and logic. He has already made the emotional connection in understanding that white nationalist ideology hurts humans he cares about, and in Europe he performs the research to renounce the logic of white nationalism. Through analysis of historical texts and architecture, he reasons that much of what he previously believed is incorrect, which leads him to disavow much of what he previously accepted as established science.

21. "Out there in the massive crowd were thousands of Tea Partyers and several lawmakers they continued to support, like Ted Cruz, Jeff Sessions, and Steve King, all of whom had signed a pledge to defeat any bill resembling amnesty for immigrants. 'It's like I helped feed a monster that won't go back into the cage,' Derek

told Allison once. 'I can't go back and do everything over.' But Allison continued to insist there *was* something he could do. 'You need to make these points in public,' she told him. 'You've caused too much damage to slip away.'" (Chapter 9, Page 207)

For Derek and Allison, it is not enough that he personally, privately renounces white nationalism. For Derek's own future and for the benefit of the nation, they believe Derek must publicly decry the ideology. Derek spent most of his life leading white nationalism to prominence. He has abandoned the ideology, but the harm he caused persists. Derek and Allison believe a public denunciation of white nationalism is the only way to fix some of the damage he has caused.

22. "If he was going to go through the painful process of renouncing his beliefs, he wanted to [...] apologize for the damage he caused and condemn racism in the most public way he could. He wanted to release a thorough statement and then legally change his name, switching his first and middle names, so he could leave Florida for his first semester at Western Michigan and begin anew as Roland Derek Black. But there was no way to condemn his own views and actions without also condemning his family's views and actions. He was sure they would be upset, and likely furious. What he didn't know was whether they would ever speak to him again." (Chapter 9, Pages 211-12)

Derek now believes a public denunciation of white nationalism is necessary, both for his own future and for the nation, to rectify wrongs he perpetuated. If Derek wants a future divorced from white nationalism, he must put on the public record that he no longer espouses the ideology and must legally change his name so his identity is divorced from white nationalism. He carefully crafts his message, hoping to convey his complete abandonment of white nationalism, offer a thorough critique of the ideology, apologize to those hurt by his past, and maintain a positive relationship with his family. As much as his relationship with white nationalism is rooted in his relationship with his family, his relationship with his family is rooted in white nationalism. Family and white nationalism are inseparable concepts in the Black household. If you remove white nationalism, you remove family.

23. "By the end of the night, Don felt reassured about the possibilities of white nationalism. 'Camaraderie heals the spirit,' Don remembered thinking of that night, and he continued to feel even more restored the next day, when he returned to the conference room and surveyed the people seated around him. The crowd was younger than ever before, and it included disaffected young men who had been introduced to Stormfront through online video game forums and the so-called men's rights movement, a collection of fringe misogynists who believe men have become disempowered by feminism and political correctness. Nearly half were attending their first white nationalist conference." (Chapter 12, Page 239)

Derek may have publicly denounced white nationalism, but the effects of his earlier efforts persist in the movement. The Stormfront conference has a higher attendance than any white nationalism conference Don previously attended, and the audience is younger than ever before. Derek's message and the political climate reach many disaffected young white males. The movement has grown beyond Derek, Don, or even Duke.

24. "[I]n Trump's speech, Don heard echoes of a strategy that he and Duke had pioneered together thirty-five years earlier when they tried to rehabilitate the Klan's image by shifting its focus from cross burnings in the Deep South to rallies against illegal immigration on the California border. Duke started the Klan Border Watch in 1977, and for two weeks he drove around the desert with binoculars and a few hundred other Klan members while the national news media trailed behind them. 'This isn't an issue about race or prejudice,' Duke insisted back then. He said securing the border was about protecting America's culture and its economy. And so, on behalf of the Klan in the late 1970s, Duke proposed the idea of building a wall, much as Trump was suggesting now." (Chapter 12, Page 249)

Current Republican messaging on illegal immigration and building a wall along the United States' southern border with Mexico originated as Ku Klux Klan talking points crafted by Don and Duke in the 1970s. Since then Don, Duke, Derek, and others have refined the verbiage to make the message more palatable to mainstream white America, but the messaging originated from white supremacists in the Ku Klux Klan as a dog whistle for racist policy.

25. "For three decades white nationalist leaders like Don, Duke, and Derek had been smoothing their extremist message to make it more palatable to the far conservative Right—removing their hoods, eliminating slurs, refining their rhetoric, mastering the internet. And now, for the first time in Don's memory, a major presidential candidate had started calling out in their direction with one dog whistle after another, until suddenly Trump and the white nationalist movement were close enough to wink at each other across the

internet, or sometimes even hold hands." (Chapter 12, Pages 250-51)

Trump is the political embodiment of Derek's ideas. Derek believes that Trump successfully employs his strategies to bring white nationalism into mainstream acceptance, or at least successfully attach himself to the movement, and takes the ideology into the White House. A master at marketing and public relations, Trump uses every technique that Don, Duke, and Derek pioneered to communicate with the white nationalist community in dog whistles, to let them know he is on their team while achieving mainstream acceptance. Trump also illustrates in his electoral victory what Derek knew all along: There are more white nationalists and white nationalist sympathizers than anyone realized, and when they lose belief in their economic security, they revert to white separatism to maintain their privileged societal position.

ESSAY TOPICS

1. To what extent did Derek's upbringing influence his white supremacist ideology? To what extent is he himself responsible for his ideology?

2. Even before his transformation, Derek treated all people with respect in personal interactions, even if his ideology dismissed or reduced them as people. How is this at odds with Derek's public statements about his ideology? How does this comport with Derek's public statements about his ideology?

3. Assess Matthew's nonjudgmental inclusion approach to reforming Derek. Would you have taken the same approach? If so, is there anything you would have done differently? If not, what approach would you have taken and why?

4. What single factor most influenced Derek to abandon his white supremacist ideology? What other factors motivated Derek?

5. Explain how a combination of approaches to Derek by his classmates influenced his transformation over time. Explain how different approaches worked together and how conflicting approaches may have hurt each other.

6. How has family influenced Derek's ideology? What role does Derek's family play in his ideological transformation? How has Derek's nonfamily community, both white nationalist and at college, influenced his ideology? What role does that community play in his ideological transformation?

7. How has Derek's ideological transformation affected his college friends? How has his transformation affected his biological family? How has his transformation affected the white nationalist community and larger movement?

8. Derek has been publicly speaking against white nationalism for several years. To what extent has he erased the wrongs he's done? Is there a way for Derek to fully atone for his actions as a white nationalist?

9. Don and Duke embody the white nationalist movement. For many years, they were the movement's two public representatives. What does it say about the movement that Don chooses white nationalism over his son? What does it say about Derek that he strives to continue a relationship with his family, even though he finds their ideology abhorrent?

10. The book ends with Derek saying to Don that the nation is approaching a critical moment in its racial struggle. Do you think the nation has reached that critical moment? Why, or why not? If not, do you believe the critical moment is coming? Provide evidence.